Yes, Let's Compromise on Abortion

--By Laurel Federbush

2

Today I did a Google search with the words "abortion" and "compromise." All I could find were articles from people on both sides about how you can't compromise on abortion. No way, no how. There was nothing to steer me in the direction of anyone trying to arrive at any kind of compromise on the abortion issue, which is what I had set out trying to find.

I'm sure there are such people. Years ago I heard talk show host Laura Ingraham ridiculing a priest for having a website encouraging discussion on the subject of abortion. She was offended that a priest's site would allow pro-choice views. Then she ended up throwing her support behind Donald Trump, who had been pro-choice until midway through his campaign for president, which somehow made sense to her. Trump wasn't the subject of her scorn, but a priest encouraging respectful dialog was.

There must be others seeking compromise, even on such an

inflammatory wedge issue, but they're hard to find. When we do find such voices, though, we ought to heed them.

Yes, we should compromise on abortion. It's not a message you'll hear very often. Anyone trying to start a dialogue is likely to be drowned out by the voices on both sides shouting, "No way in Hell!" Those on the pro-choice side accuse their opponents of wanting to enslave women, while those on the pro-life side liken their opponents to those perpetrating the Holocaust. If your opponent is pure evil, why should you compromise with him or her? To give an inch would be like selling your soul.

And there are those who say that, no matter how desirable it might be, finding a compromise on abortion is just impossible. You either believe this or you believe that. There is no middle ground, so don't even try to find it.

Abortion isn't like any other issue. It isn't just a matter of choice, like deciding between a red shirt or a blue one, since a human life (or potential life) is at stake. And it isn't like the Holocaust or any other type of genocide because, among other things, in no other example does one human live inside another. Abortion is an issue unto itself.

And it's not an issue where you can decide it, once and for all, or put an end to it—it's ongoing, as long as there's a woman who gets pregnant. Each case is new. Women will always want control over their own bodies. And the apparent humanity of fetuses will always compel people to oppose their destruction.

When there are two opposing sides, the sensible thing to do in many or even most situations is to compromise and try to find common ground. Why does compromising make sense? Because it's a way to get at least part of what you want. Otherwise, you're likely not to get any, and to have your opponent take an even harsher position than before just to get even, and to make sure you never rise from the dust. Compromise can also help you win new allies, if they realize you can be reasoned with and you're not their enemy. If you can understand their position, they may be more receptive to yours. Compromise also preserves the peace. No compromise leads to actual war. Our country has already had one civil war—don't think we couldn't have another.

There are good people on both sides of the abortion issue. If you don't know someone you respect on the other side, you really need to get out more. It could be a friend or family member, or multiple people. Maybe even most of the people you know. Do you really think they're all evil?

Personally, I'm pro-life, but I wasn't always. I was pro-choice most of my life, but came into contact with pro-lifers who changed the way I saw things. I didn't change my mind immediately, it was a gradual process. People's minds can change. There are other people who were once pro-life and for one reason or another changed their minds about the issue and are now vehemently pro-choice. It can happen.

There are people (one of my rabbis, among them) who object to the terms "pro-life" and "pro-choice" as simplistic. They are simplistic terms. Everything about the abortion controversy is presented in simplistic terms. Slogans and bumper stickers. But it isn't a simple issue, and never can be. I am going to use those terms precisely because they are simple. But that doesn't mean they tell the full story.

According to surveys, most Americans support legal abortion but with some restrictions. That's sort of a middle ground, legal with some restrictions. Not everyone would agree on which restrictions, but it's a moderating principle that some restrictions would exist. And maybe we don't all agree that abortion should be legal; or we don't all agree that there should be any restrictions. But that's the point of a compromise—it's something reasonably in the middle, where each side gets some of what they want. Neither side in the current abortion debate represents any kind of middle ground. Pro-choice advocates used to say that abortion should be "safe, legal, and rare." They now leave out "rare." Roe v. Wade was actually a moderating ruling, since it recognized that the fetus becomes more developed during the later stages of pregnancy, and makes fetal viability grounds for its protection. Pro-lifers may be wrong to reject Roe v. Wade, which doesn't offer protection to a non-viable fetus. But pro-choicers are now offering up bills that offer no protection even to viable fetuses. So I would suggest that pro-lifers embrace Roe v. Wade and challenge those bills on the grounds that they are inconsistent with Roe v. Wade.

There are many possible types of compromise. Here are some examples:

Let abortion be legal, but only at the earliest stages, except in cases of life/health of the mother.

Let abortion be legal only at the earliest stages, except in cases of rape, incest, or life/health of the mother.

Let abortion be legal only in the earliest stages, except in cases of rape, incest, or life/health of the mother but make free birth control easily accessible everywhere.

Let abortion be legal in any and all circumstances, but insist that abortion providers give each patient accurate information about fetal development; and information about adoption and social service agencies for pregnant women and mothers.

Let abortion be legal in any and all circumstances, but require that abortion providers show the mother an ultrasound of the fetus.

Let abortion be legal in any and all circumstances, but require abortion providers to drop the intentionally-dehumanizing terminology and instead talk about unborn or pre-born babies.

Let abortion be legal in any and all circumstances, and provide many more social services for pregnant women and mothers, including universal childcare.

Let abortion be legal in some or all circumstances, but study what leads to lower abortion rates and enact any such measures.

Or, any combination of the above.

Some of those I might find more palatable than others, but no one is going to get everything they want in a compromise.

Don't get me wrong—I can be just as loud and strident about my opinions on abortion as anyone. You can find me in numerous heated arguments about it on Facebook. And I may engage in more tonight or tomorrow. Passionate beliefs make it hard to discuss things in a calm, reasoned way. But our leaders and would-be leaders would be wise to help us with moderation, for the sake of holding our country together.

Moderation can be smart politics, too, even though you don't often hear that on this issue. Say I'm a pro-choice politician. Why shouldn't I go as pro-abortion as possible? Because most people are somewhere in the middle when it comes to abortion. And there are some anti-abortion people who aren't single-issue voters who, if not enchanted by your opponent, might consider voting for you if there's even a glimmer of respect for the sanctity of life in your position. Or, say I'm a pro-life politician. Why not be as extreme in my defense of the unborn as humanly possible? If you don't want women to have abortions, you might not want to go around alienating women by leaving them out of the equation. If women are convinced that you're the enemy of their right to choose, why will they listen to anything you have to say? And why should they vote for you instead of lobbying against you? Plus, both of you—ultra-anti-abortion and ultra-pro-abortion politicians—are energizing your opponents. Making them stronger.

Abortion isn't a left-right issue, even though those dividing us would like it to be. There are people of all political stripes on both sides of the debate. And maybe I'm wrong to talk about "both sides," since it's a complex issue with many sides. Life experience, religious beliefs, sexuality, and social awareness mean that none of us will see it quite the same way. Realizing that it's a complex issue, not just a Democrat vs. Republican, or liberal vs. conservative, type of thing would make it harder for the people who would like to use it as a wedge issue to divide us to do so.

The opinion of when life begins is different for different religions. Making the abortion issue a question of that makes it into a religious war. There are certainly people who would like to stir up such a war, but I would hope most of us aren't among them. There have been other cases in the past where an issue that was supposedly about one thing was really about something else. The Nazis used the issue of animal welfare as a way to persecute Jewish butchers.

Circumcision opponents may not be the least bit anti-Semitic, but their arguments often serve an anti-Semitic purpose. As a pro-life Jew, I'm torn. I believe that the pro-life side is most consistent with Jewish values, although the overwhelming majority of Jews are pro-choice. Still, I can see this issue being used as a way to impose a Christian theological view on everyone. Jews generally believe that the baby becomes a person separate from the mother once it's born. (I recently heard from a rabbi that there is a Jewish position against partial-birth abortion, but that may not be widely known.) Even though I'm pro-life, I'm realizing that some of the anti-abortion rhetoric may actually be a subtle way to keep alive a pernicious anti-Semitic canard, the "blood libel" about Jews being baby-killers. It turns out that Jews have a lower abortion rate than some Christian faiths; still, if a Christian view of when life begins is imposed on everyone, then everyone who has a different view can be seen as a baby-killer and subject to religious persecution. At the same time, forcing Christians who hold a view that life begins at conception to participate in what to them is murder could be another kind of religious persecution. Tolerance for different views is necessary for a pluralistic society. And no view of when life begins is inherently more or less scientific than any other.

And on the subject of religion: you may be saying, "I can't accept an abortion law that doesn't

square with my religious beliefs."
If your religious view is that a
human being exists and has rights
from the moment of conception,
how could you tolerate any law
that doesn't recognize that? The
thing is, you tolerate laws that
don't recognize that all the time
without flinching. In fact, in no
other context do you demand that
a fetus be treated as a separate
human being. Not for purposes of
the census, of taxation, of
government representation, of
welfare benefits...only when it
comes to abortion. Which may be
reasonable, since the right to life is
the most basic human right. But

the inconsistency may be noted
nonetheless. Or, if you're Jewish,
you may be saying, "My religion
teaches that life begins at birth."
Actually, the religious view in
Judaism is that a baby isn't fully
human until it has survived 30 days
outside the womb. This may have
been arrived at for pragmatic
reasons, since originally there were
so many miscarriages and deaths
of newborns that funeral rites just
weren't remotely practical in each
instance. But you won't see any
modern Jews insisting that a
newborn baby isn't a person. So
clearly Jews are comfortable with a
legal stance on the beginning of

life which is different from their traditional religious view. The point is, our laws aren't totally consistent with anyone's religious beliefs, and maybe they shouldn't be. This isn't a theocracy. We compromise all the time. It's called civilization.

Both sides of the debate are sometimes guilty of hypocrisy. Some of the same people arguing against abortion are the very ones who are first to stigmatize unmarried women who find themselves pregnant. And some of those who are most pro-choice when it comes to abortion are less so when it comes to the choice to have a lot of children.

Which reminds me of a thought I had, that anti-abortion people may do well to advocate a staunchly pro-choice view, because coercive population control measures are spreading to other countries besides China, and may soon make it to our shores. One of my pro-life ideas is that abortion isn't just a nobody-else's-business thing, because taking the life of an unborn baby deprives all of us of that unique individual and his or her descendants. But I also recognize that declaring that the state has an interest in a reproductive decision is something that could just as easily be used to compel abortion as to forbid it. One area where pro-life and pro-choice people can certainly find common ground is in opposing coercive state population control. It would be good to see deliberate efforts for people on both sides to collaborate on this.

Those are some of my thoughts, and I may have said all the wrong things and not convinced anyone of anything. But the idea is for it to be a discussion about finding common ground, or at least listening respectfully to things we disagree with and then having our say. And for an end to the self-righteousness that too often plagues this issue, that I'm just as guilty of as anyone.

People who have actually been pregnant and had children or have had abortions obviously know things that the rest of us don't, and that needs to be acknowledged by everyone. But other people have insights and experiences, too. Whose opinion should we value more, that of a woman who realized she needed to have an abortion, or that of a worker at an abortion clinic who realized that what they were doing was wrong? Both speak from experience. I know that men are often told that their opinions don't matter, but I don't see how that can be a feminist position when we want men to be just as involved in their children's lives as the mothers— who these days would say that

raising a child is women's work?
And then there's the idea that it
takes a village to raise a child.
Then let's respect what the entire
village has to say before the child is
born, too. All the while
recognizing that, regardless of the
law, it ends up being the woman's
decision.

Pro-choice people are right
that pro-lifers want to ban
abortion completely, or with few
exceptions. And pro-lifers are right
that pro-choicers promote
abortion as perfectly acceptable at

all stages of pregnancy for any reason. While you or I may agree with one of those positions, neither is where most Americans are, and neither one is a compromise position. Furthermore, those positions are counterproductive, since pro-choicers will reject any regulation for fear of losing all reproductive rights; and pro-lifers will refuse any acknowledgment of the woman's right to make her own reproductive decisions. And I see single-issue voters throwing themselves behind people totally unworthy because it's the only way for them to have their views on this important subject represented.

So, let's talk about abortion, not in an "I'm right and you're wrong" way but really listening to what the other person has to say. And no name-calling, please. No one has a monopoly on facts or on morality. Let's find something— anything—that we agree on, and cling to that, instead of the myriad issues where we disagree. People of good will can come together to solve problems. I don't know how much luck any of us will have with arriving at a compromise, but we aren't even trying. And that's wrong. We are all entitled to our beliefs, and we may be right to be repelled by the actions of the other side. Fine. But through respectful dialog we can make things better.

Getting laws passed that reflect our own beliefs may be Pyrrhic victories. As a pro-lifer, I rejoice when strict anti-abortion laws are passed. But I can't ignore that these laws are extremely unpopular, inspiring fear in women and doing nothing to convince

them to choose life. I'm sure pro-
choicers rejoice when the most lax
laws doing away with any
restrictions on abortion are
passed, but then they find
themselves having to defend or
deny the extremes that would be
allowed. Even if you or I might
agree with a law, that doesn't
mean that the law would
ultimately help the cause we are
supporting.

I may be on Facebook
tomorrow posting inflammatory
things about this issue—

sometimes I get really into that. But I think it would be more constructive if I could help, in any small way, to bring about a willingness for both sides to compromise.

Thank you.